Teaching Handbook for the Interactive Mathematics Program

I M P ™

A Teacher-to-Teacher Guide
by Lori Green

This material is based upon work supported by the National Science Foundation under award number ESI-9255262. Any opinions, findings, and conclusions or recommendations expressed in this publication are those of the authors and do not necessarily reflect the views of the National Science Foundation.

Key Curriculum Press
1150 65th Street
Emeryville, California 94608
editorial@keypress.com
http://www.keypress.com

10 9 8 7 6 5 4   05 04 03 02 01
ISBN 1-55953-256-4
Printed in the United States of America

Editor
Casey FitzSimons

Editorial Assistants
Caroline Ayres, Jeff Gammon

Advisors for the Interactive Mathematics Program
Dan Fendel, Diane Resek, Sherry Fraser, Lynne Alper

Reviewers
Mary Jo Cittadino, Don Cruser, Donna Gaarder, Sandie Gilliam, Dan Johnson, Jean Klanica

Publisher
Steven Rasmussen

Editorial Director
John Bergez

Acknowledgments

The IMP Teacher Advisory Group

Dean Ballard
Mission High School
San Francisco, CA

Carolyn Barth
Tracy Joint Union High School
Tracy, CA

Larry Biggers
Highlands High School,
San Antonio, TX

Libby Berry
Silver Creek High School
San Jose, CA

Matt Bremer
Berkeley High School
Berkeley, CA

Janice Bussey
Tracy Joint Union High School
Tracy, CA

Greg Cotton
Grant High School
Portland, OR

Margaret DeArmond
East Bakersfield High School
Bakersfield, CA

Sandy Douglass
Grant High School
Portland, OR

Eileen Favalora
Tracy Joint Union High School
Tracy, CA

Valorie Fayfich
Lanier High School
San Antonio, TX

Donna Gaarder
Tracy Joint Union High School
Tracy, CA

Lori Green
Tracy Joint Union High School
Tracy, CA

Philippe Henri
Berkeley High School
Berkeley, CA

Theresa Hernandez-Heinz
Mission High School
San Francisco, CA

Byron Hildebrand
Highlands High School
San Antonio, TX

Steve Jenkins
Eaglecrest High School
Aurora, CO

Dan Johnson
Silver Creek High School
San Jose, CA

George Kirchner
Tracy Joint Union High School
Tracy, CA

Jean Klanica
Eaglecrest High School
Aurora, CO

Barbara Knox
Grant High School
Portland, OR

Jim Luhring
Eaglecrest High School
Aurora, CO

Susan Malberg
Berkeley High School
Berkeley, CA

Tony Mana
Mission High School
San Francisco, CA

Leigh Ann McCready
Live Oak High School
Morgan Hill, CA

Reuben Miller
Beacon High School
Oakland, CA

Fred Rectanus
Grant High School
Portland, OR

Robin Rice
Tyee High School
Seattle, WA

Dennis Ross
Mission High School
San Francisco, CA

Barbara Schallau
Silver Creek High School
San Jose, CA

Linda Schroers
Tracy Joint Union High School
Tracy, CA

Frank Slaton
Silver Creek High School
San Jose, CA

Greg Smith
Tracy Joint Union High School
Tracy, CA

Nancy Springer
Beacon High School
Oakland, CA

Cathie Thompson
East Bakersfield High School
Bakersfield, CA

Becky Troutman
Tracy Joint Union High School
Tracy, CA

Jim Tucker
Grant High School
Portland, OR

Kathryn Wallentine
Tyee High School
Seattle, WA

Jack Withrow
Tyee High School
Seattle, WA

Margaret Wong
Berkeley High School
Berkeley, CA

Judy Wright
Lanier High School
San Antonio, TX

Sue Yabuki
Grant High School
Portland, OR

Adrienne Yank
Berkeley High School
Berkeley, CA

Tom Zimmerman
Mission High School
San Francisco, CA

About Lori Green

Lori Green brings the supplies for *Shadows* experiments into her classroom at Lincoln High School in Stockton, California.

Lori Green was one of the original pilot teachers of the Interactive Mathematics Program curriculum at Tracy Joint Union High School in Tracy, California, in 1989. As National Teaching Coordinator, she has observed hundreds of IMP classrooms, led IMP workshops, participated in the development and revision of the curriculum, and given guidance to IMP teachers throughout the country.

Contents

Preface: Welcome to an Adventure!

Welcome to a teaching adventure. By choosing to teach the curriculum developed by the Interactive Mathematics Program (IMP), you are making a commitment to hard work for the sake of young people's mathematics education. Bringing about change will not be easy, but you will have the reward of seeing your students grow as thinkers and communicators as well as mathematicians!

Since 1989, I have been teaching this curriculum and visiting IMP classrooms. My experiences watching colleagues at work have confirmed my belief that all students can learn mathematics. I've had the good fortune to travel throughout the country, from Hawaii to Washington, DC, and many places in between. Along the way, many IMP classroom teachers have shared their practical tips for making this program achieve the maximum benefit, and this handbook includes many of those tips. Since it's impossible for me to trace specific ideas to individual teachers, I will simply say a hearty "Thank you" to all who welcomed me into their classrooms, participated with me at workshops, and shared their insights with me. I have included some anecdotes in the voices of some of the pioneer IMP teachers, and I want to thank them for their contributions to this document.

The IMP curriculum was developed with underlying principles that are evident throughout the curriculum. This handbook presents a brief introduction to these principles, and we hope it will assist you in implementing those principles. Keep in mind, though, that a document such as this cannot replace the valuable ideas and experiences gained through collaboration among teachers within the school setting and at inservice workshops. The Interactive Mathematics Program strongly recommends that schools implementing this curriculum institute a full-scale program of professional development. Only through such a program will teachers have the support they deserve as they do the hard work of learning both new mathematics and new teaching strategies.

Lori Green

A Brief IMP History

In 1989, the National Council of Teachers of Mathematics (NCTM) published *Curriculum and Evaluation Standards for School Mathematics*, which called for major reforms in mathematics education, including

- a shift from a skill-centered to a problem-centered curriculum

- a broadening of the scope of the secondary curriculum to include such areas as statistics, probability, and discrete mathematics

- changes in pedagogical strategies, including emphasis on communication and writing skills

- expansion of the pool of students that receives a "core" mathematical education

The Interactive Mathematics Program (IMP) is a collaboration by mathematicians, teacher-educators, and teachers who have been working together since 1989. Together, we have developed a new four-year high school mathematics curriculum to embody the vision of NCTM's *Standards*. This curriculum is intended to replace the traditional program of Algebra I, Geometry, Algebra II/Trigonometry, and Precalculus.

The first three years of the IMP curriculum were pilot-tested during 1989–92 at Berkeley High School in Berkeley, CA; Mission High School in San Francisco, CA; and Tracy Joint Union High School in Tracy, CA. The fourth year of the curriculum was pilot-tested during 1993–94 at Berkeley High School; Mission High School; Eaglecrest High School in Aurora, CO; and Silver Creek High School in San Jose, CA.

All of the curriculum has undergone several rounds of review and revision. Throughout both the initial development and the revision, the writers worked directly with teachers and sat with groups of students in IMP classes, discovering what worked and what didn't. The final materials are the result of field testing with hundreds of teachers, thousands of classrooms, and myriad students.

Evaluation and follow-up studies show that IMP students have been admitted to first-rate colleges throughout the country and are doing well. They have scored at least as well on standardized tests as students from traditional programs, and they are also learning topics that students in traditional programs do not see at all. Students have transferred successfully both into and out of the IMP curriculum.

What Is an IMP Unit?

A New Look for the Curriculum

The IMP curriculum probably looks different from any textbook you have worked with before. Instead of being organized into courses called Algebra, Geometry, and Trigonometry, it comes in "units" that are part of each "year" of the program.

That's because the IMP curriculum is integrated and problem-centered. Most units begin with a central problem that is explored and solved over the course of six to eight weeks. As you guide students through a variety of smaller problems within the unit, they develop the mathematical concepts and techniques they need to solve the central problem. A particular unit may combine several branches of mathematics so that students see how important ideas are related to each other.

Some of these central problems are based in practical real-world situations, such as maximizing profits for a business or studying population growth. Others are more fanciful, involving situations like a pennant race or a circus act. Central problems may have connections with history, science, or literature. Because the curriculum is organized around such "big problems," students get a rich look at how mathematics is actually used—a feature that is often lacking in traditional textbooks.

The Student Text

The student text contains the mathematics assignments and activities through which students develop the concepts and skills of each unit. It also contains reference material on major new ideas and a glossary of important terms.

Basic assignments

There are three main types of student assignments:

- In-class activities
- Daily homework
- Problems of the Week (POWs)

Generally speaking, students will examine new concepts through an in-class activity. By starting in class, students have each other as resources. You are there to provide guidance and direction as they begin their exploration.

In homework assignments, students reinforce and extend concepts that are introduced in class and sometimes explore new ideas. Some of these assignments provide opportunities for students to reflect on and synthesize what they have learned over a longer period of time.

Problems of the Week (POWs) let students explore mathematical ideas without the constraints and time pressure of needing to know something tomorrow or next week. These are open-ended problems, often mathematical classics, that cannot be solved easily in a very short period of time. In POW write-ups, students describe how they worked on the problem and explain their reasoning; these problems are a vehicle through which students improve their mathematical writing. Though POWs are embedded within the units, the mathematics of these problems is usually independent of the unit problem.

Supplemental problems

Each student unit also includes a collection of supplemental problems, both for reinforcement of concepts and skills and for extending ideas beyond the basic curriculum. These problems provide you with a way to tailor the curriculum to the needs of individual students. The special role of supplemental problems in the heterogeneous classroom is discussed later in this handbook.

A Teacher's Guide for Each Unit

For each unit, there is a teacher's guide that explains in detail how to present the material of the unit. This guide organizes the material as a series of daily lesson plans; it discusses how the mathematical concepts should evolve from the student activities and discussions. The guide suggests specific hints you can give or questions you can ask to promote student dialogue, and provides additional mathematical background for your reference. It also contains specific suggestions as to how you can use the supplemental problems.

Overview

Each teacher's guide begins with an overview that gives a summary of the unit, a list of the main concepts and skills that students will be learning, a description of any special materials you will need to provide, and specific grading suggestions for the unit.

Collegial support

Because this curriculum represents a major change for most teachers, you should look to your colleagues for support as much as possible. The developers of IMP recommend that as teachers present each year of the curriculum for the first time, they have a common preparation period in which to discuss their achievements, frustrations, and questions. In many schools, teachers have been provided with an *extra* preparation period for this professional sharing.

Teachers around the country have described this type of collegial support as one of the most useful forms of professional development in their teaching careers. I certainly know how valuable and productive this time was for me when I began teaching the IMP curriculum. Each teacher's guide includes suggested topics—geared to the specific issues of the unit—for you to discuss with your colleagues during this shared time.

A Complete Four-Year Curriculum

This four-year curriculum includes the fundamental ideas that have been part of the high school syllabus since before we went to school—concepts and skills from algebra, geometry, and trigonometry. Although this material is organized in a new way and embedded in problem-based units, the key ideas are all there and students will use them and revisit them throughout the four years. The individual units of the curriculum are described in an Appendix to this handbook.

In addition to this traditional material, students will also learn about branches of mathematics, such as statistics or matrix algebra, that are new to the high school curriculum but are used throughout business and industry today. These additions to the mathematics content of the curriculum are consistent with the recommendations of NCTM's *Standards*.

By combining traditional concepts and newer material in an integrated setting, the IMP curriculum meets the needs of both college-bound students and those headed directly into the workforce. By putting these ideas in context, the curriculum prepares students to use problem-solving skills both in school and on the job.

An Active and Engaging Approach to Learning

The Need for Change

Educators have often lamented that the majority of students do not understand mathematical concepts, or see why mathematical procedures work, or know when to use a given mathematical technique. According to the National Research Council's *Everybody Counts,* "Much of the failure in school mathematics is due to a tradition of teaching that is inappropriate to the way students learn."[1]

In the traditional teaching model that has dominated our schools for many years, a teacher demonstrates an algorithm or technique, assigns a set of problems for students to do on their own, and then tests the students a week later on their accumulation of skills.

Students in such a situation often do not understand what they are doing because they are simply following instructions. They typically see no need for the mathematics, other than to pass the test. The result is a system in which students "view mathematics as a rigid system of externally dictated rules, governed by standards of accuracy, speed, and memory."[2]

The solution to this dilemma lies in active student engagement in learning.

> Research in learning shows that students actually construct their own understanding based on new experiences that enlarge the intellectual framework in which ideas can be created. . . . Mathematics becomes useful to a student only when it has been developed through a personal intellectual engagement that creates new understanding.[3]

---

[1] National Research Council, *Everybody Counts: A Report to the Nation on the Future of Mathematics Education* (Washington, DC, National Academy Press, 1989), p. 6.
[2] *Everybody Counts,* p. 44.
[3] *Everybody Counts,* p. 6.

This process of "personal intellectual engagement" lies at the heart of IMP's view of learning and is shared by educators around the world. NCTM's *Curriculum and Evaluation Standards* elaborates on what this means in terms of what should happen in the classroom:

> Students should be exposed to numerous and various interrelated experiences that encourage them to value the mathematics enterprise, to develop mathematical habits of mind, and to understand the role of mathematics in human affairs; . . . they should be encouraged to explore, to guess, and even to make and correct errors so that they gain confidence in their ability to solve complex problems; . . . they should read, write, and discuss mathematics; and . . . they should conjecture, test, and build arguments about a conjecture's validity.[4]

An approach to learning that maximizes student involvement in thinking through important mathematical issues leads to a different role for the teacher. It deemphasizes the teacher's role as creator of concepts and disseminator of algorithms, and sees the teacher more as a facilitator of learning. The teacher provides learning opportunities, asks thought-provoking questions, and allows students to develop their own mathematical frameworks. The teacher uses his or her expertise to provide the "glue" needed to help students tie ideas together and to clarify any misconceptions that may arise. The teacher no longer dictates which steps students will take to solve a problem. An approach which promotes lifelong learning combines the mathematics at hand with thinking and reasoning skills, and encourages risk-taking and perseverance.

IMP Promotes Understanding

The Interactive Mathematics Program lets students be active, engaged learners, using what they already know, making conjectures and learning from errors. The IMP curriculum presents students with rich mathematical contexts and gives them well-designed opportunities to discover and develop mathematical concepts as well as to prove important results. This approach offers students meaning for abstract concepts, gives them ownership of mathematical ideas, and heightens their interest in mathematics. Research shows that IMP students are apt to take more mathematics in high school than their peers in traditional programs.

---

[4] *Curriculum and Evaluation Standards for School Mathematics* (Reston, VA: National Council of Teachers of Mathematics, 1989), p. 5.

Josie: "Josie was a tenth grader, with a shallow math background but good verbal test scores. She came into IMP to understand math—the Whys and Hows. Josie came back to talk to us after her first semester in college. She talked to my seniors and told them about her first traditional math class in three years. She said, 'I always ask questions. The others don't. I thought it was because they knew it already, but then after class they would ask me questions. I realized that they are just scared to ask. They don't know what is going on. Oh yes, I got an A.'" — Byron Hildebrand, Highlands H.S., San Antonio, Texas

How to Promote Mathematical Thinking

We teachers were most likely taught mathematics in a system where mastery of skills was the focus. We were the ones who succeeded in that system. IMP is not based on a mastery approach to learning. While the IMP curriculum seeks to attain the same goal of long-term mathematical understanding as mastery approaches, IMP promotes that understanding through a series of spiraled mathematics experiences which result over time in mathematical proficiency. It may be exceptionally hard for us to let go of the idea that students take more responsibility for their own learning. You will have to remind yourself, often, that you are trying to build independent thinkers and reasoners. As you see your students struggling with an awkward approach to a problem, you may have to work hard to keep from giving them the most elegant way. Easier said than done!

For the IMP teacher who finds it hard to let go of his or her traditional role in the classroom, my number one piece of advice is: *Be patient!* Have faith in the students and have faith in the curriculum. Your students are creative and capable! You will be surprised and delighted by the variety of ways students attack problems and investigations, yet come to successful conclusions, when given the opportunity to think independently and together. You will have to bite your tongue as you watch a student play with a topic for which you know the conventional super-formula. Don't steal that student's "Ah-ha!" experience.

Developing knowledge experientially with an activity-oriented curriculum takes more time than "delivering" knowledge through lecture. Think about why that is true. A student developing his or her own mathematical ideas to solve a challenging problem has to do many things—see a need for the math, try a problem with tools already at hand, look for a pattern, investigate a conjecture, and convince himself or herself of the findings. Of course that takes more time—it is a much longer process than listening to a lecture and practicing an algorithm. The *process* is what gives the student ownership of the end result.

Although you don't want to steal the "Ah-ha's," that doesn't mean that you sit by idly and let your expertise go to waste. You, as the facilitator for the learning process, have to be a skilled questioner. For example, as groups begin work on a problem, you will need to ensure that they understand the directions so that all students can access the problem. Perhaps you will have one student read the directions aloud and then have groups paraphrase them. Once kids get started, you will want to walk around the room asking questions of all kinds—*probing questions* to promote thought, *testing questions* to see where the students are, and *focusing questions* to have students explain or justify their ideas. The teacher's guide for each unit includes samples of such questions for you to use in the context of specific problems and activities.

Your Own Growth

As you watch your students become active and engaged learners, you will most likely be learning yourself. Be open and share your own learning experiences with your students. If you were trained in a different school of thought, you will grow from seeing the various approaches that students offer. You will also benefit from attending teacher inservices which give you opportunities to learn as your IMP students are learning—through exploring, questioning, guessing, estimating, arguing, and proving. As you begin each IMP unit and activity, take time to talk with at least one of your fellow IMP teachers. Together, identify the goals of the unit or activity and think through how you are going to assess student progress toward such goals and grade student performance.

Collaborative Learning and Groups

The IMP curriculum is designed so that much of the in-class learning takes place as students work together collaboratively in randomly formed groups. This group work is balanced by opportunities for students to work individually.

This section discusses the reasons for the collaborative approach to learning, the process of forming groups, and ways to make collaborative learning work successfully in your classroom.

Why Group Work?

In a traditional mathematics classroom, each student sits at a separate desk and works alone, interacting only with the teacher. Looking at someone else's work is considered cheating. Consequently, many people see mathematics as something to be done in isolation. They believe that if you want to work with people, you do not go into mathematics.

In reality, collaboration is just as necessary in mathematics as it is in other aspects of society. Genuine mathematical work, whether done by mathematicians, plumbers, engineers, or dental hygienists, typically involves collaboration and communication. Indeed, employers identify the ability to work with others as one of the most important skills they look for in job applicants. The IMP curriculum teaches students how to collaborate by having them work together, usually in groups of four.

Students can learn a great deal by working collaboratively with others. Here are some of the many benefits of group work:

- Students working in groups get to see different approaches to a given problem. Varied approaches to a problem lead to added insight and increased understanding. As students hear each other's approaches, they can ask questions to clarify the ideas.

- Small groups create a safe environment for students to take risks and make mistakes. A student is more likely to ask a question or take a risk in a group of four than in a class of thirty-six.

- When students are in small groups, more of them get to participate in discussions and carry out experiments. A task for four people allows each member to participate, whereas a question or problem thrown out to a whole class will probably get responses from at most a few students.

- In a group, students take the responsibility for each other's work habits and classroom behavior. The students see their groups as somewhat like families, in which it is each member's job to support and keep tabs on the others. This allows the teacher to be more of a facilitator.

- Through the use of randomly assigned groups, students get to work with others outside of their social groups. This promotes appreciation for, or at least an awareness of, people's differences.

How to Form Groups

One way you can create random groups is with playing cards. For example, if you have 32 students in a class, you use the aces through the eights from a standard deck. (If your class size is not a multiple of 4, you might make one or two groups of three or five.)

Shuffle the cards and allow each student to pick one. Students then sit with those who drew the same face value (aces sit together, twos sit together, and so on). Students should record their cards' suits, because the teacher's guide often suggests assigning roles based on the suit. (For example, "Have the *heart card* student from each group present the group's findings from this investigation.")

It may be helpful to tape onto each desk or table the playing card that corresponds to each group member. Teachers have found this to be helpful in taking attendance and calling on students. One IMP teacher actually hangs the playing cards by a string from the ceiling above each student's head. That way, the teacher can easily see at a glance who has which card and which suit.

You should form new groups at the beginning of each unit. The teacher's guide for each unit suggests when to create new groups, but you may change more or less often depending on your own philosophy. Some teachers change more often so that students get a chance to work with every student in the class over the course of the year. Some teachers leave the students in their groups longer to allow them to get really comfortable with their group members.

Why Random Grouping?

Whether you use playing cards or some other tool, it is important that the method you use result in random selection and that students know they are being grouped randomly.

The Interactive Mathematics Program believes that random grouping helps eliminate the labeling and tracking that can occur in a classroom. If you try to "seed" each group with a high-achieving student or plant a less motivated student in each group, the students will figure out what is going on in about two minutes! They will know who the token "smart person" is in their group and whom they will to have to carry along. One of the beauties of the IMP curriculum is that it provides varied activities and opportunities for students. Every student should be able to shine in some area, whether his or her strength is giving presentations, motivating other group members, or sharing unique problem-solving skills.

Facilitating Successful Groups

Once the students are seated in their groups and ready to go, it is up to you to run your class in a way that maximizes the benefits of collaborative learning. You will have to structure your class to ensure that students *use* their fellow group members.

This is one of the greatest challenges for any teacher; your ability to meet it will increase from unit to unit. Here are some suggestions from experienced IMP teachers:

- Make sure students consult each other before asking you a question. One IMP teacher has the motto "Ask three before you ask me!" posted on her classroom wall.

- If a group is stuck or off task, ask a thought-provoking, open question to get them going. Even better, have the students generate questions to get themselves back on task.

- Instead of brainstorming about a problem as a whole class, have group members brainstorm with each other and post their ideas on sentence strips.

- When discussing homework, have each group prepare a presentation on one part of the assignment.

- Take time periodically to have students do some reflection and discussion about the value of learning to work together.

- To show students how much you value collaborative work, incorporate the group process into students' overall grades. For example, have students assign "group participation" grades to all their group members (including themselves).

As your students become proficient in working productively as a group and become less dependent on you for guidance, congratulate yourself for creating independent learners who have gained the ability to work effectively in a collaborative setting!

The Heterogeneous Classroom

What Is Meant by *Heterogeneous?*

It seems as if you cannot read an article or attend an inservice on mathematics education reform without hearing the terms *heterogeneous classroom* and *untracking*. According to Webster's *New Collegiate Dictionary*, *heterogeneous* means "consisting of dissimilar ingredients or constituents: mixed." The movement in education is away from grouping of students by perceived ability level—tracking—and toward a heterogeneous learning environment, where students with different mathematical maturity and development levels are in the same classroom.

> Instead of helping students, sorting and tracking them according to ability institutionalize failure in mathematics. However, placing students in heterogeneous classes and groups and teaching the same old curriculum will not solve the problem. . . . The curriculum must be untracked just as the school structure must be untracked. A multidimensional curriculum will be accessible to more students and more interesting and more valuable to the most mathematically sophisticated.[5]

A heterogeneous classroom coupled with a curriculum written to engage all students creates the ideal.

Why IMP Believes in Heterogeneous Classes

Our educational system needs to broaden the range of students who learn mathematics. The heterogeneous classroom promotes access to genuine mathematics for a larger pool of students than does a system based on ability-level tracking.

---

[5] *Mathematics Framework for California Public Schools* (Sacramento, CA: California Department of Education, 1992), p. 62.

> *Kids working together: "PBS did a special on Berkeley High School, emphasizing the segregation and tracking that exist there. A student of mine told me that during a discussion in her Black Studies class about tracking and racism at BHS she raised her hand to say, 'You should come see my IMP math class. We all work together. I feel comfortable working with white kids; any kind of kid.'" —IMP student, Berkeley H.S., Berkeley, CA*

The IMP curriculum is designed to be used with heterogeneous classes, and thus to make the learning of a core mathematics curriculum more accessible, especially to those groups, such as women and minorities, who traditionally have been underrepresented in college mathematics classes and math-related fields.

A curriculum built around complex, open-ended problems can be explored at many levels of sophistication. The central problems in IMP units have a richness that will challenge the brightest student, yet their concreteness allows all students to do meaningful mathematical work.

How to Work with a Heterogeneous Class

Your Own Expectations

First on the agenda for working with a heterogeneously grouped class is to confront the expectations created in all of us by conventional conceptions of intelligence—conceptions that have led to ability-level grouping. We need to believe that *all* our students are capable of learning mathematics and, as a group, are rich in their differences.

Students' Expectations

You will probably have some students, previously identified as "gifted," who don't want to be in a class with "normal" students. You will probably also have students who have never enjoyed or succeeded in math and now feel intimidated in a class that includes all the "smart kids." In order to work with both groups, you need to convey the idea that a variety of backgrounds and learning styles will prove to be a benefit, not a detriment, to the learning process.

To take full advantage of the various learning styles and backgrounds in your IMP classroom, foster as much communication among students as possible. Provide a learning environment where students are encouraged to present their methods and ideas as well as to listen thoughtfully to the presentations of others. Provide a model, showing how to ask thoughtful questions when trying to understand another's point of view.

The heterogeneous classroom needs to provide an environment where cooperation for the common good is highly valued. Help students build an appreciation of each other's differences and encourage them to learn from other approaches and points of view.

Supplemental Problems

When you work with students who have a wide variety of math backgrounds, there may be times when discrepancies in learning arise. The supplemental problems in each unit can help you deal with these situations; they were created in response to requests from IMP teachers. These teachers asked for problems, written with the IMP style and philosophy, that could be used when students showed a need for more experience or more challenge when they approached a topic in the unit.

Using the supplemental problems often requires planning ahead. As you look over the next week of a unit, ask yourself, "Which lessons are likely to involve wide discrepancies in student response?" and "How can I meet the needs of different students?" The teacher guide will often give you guidance, since it indicates where in the unit each problem fits best.

There are two types of supplemental problems.

Reinforcements: The reinforcement problems exist for those times when your students struggle with a concept in the unit. Since they come to you from various backgrounds, some of your students may need to investigate a topic from approaches besides those provided by the basic unit. You may even find that, at some point in time, your whole class needs more work on a concept. The reinforcement problems provide such additional experience.

Extensions: There may be times when students understand a concept and want more challenge. The extension problems are provided for those who are ready to take concepts from the IMP curriculum farther than the basic unit does. Extension problems give students greater depth of understanding of topics in the current unit, rather than having them "accelerate" to material that appears later in the curriculum. In this way, they will gain appropriate challenge and enrichment and yet each new unit will be fresh for them.

Whenever you use supplemental problems, be cautious of tracking within your IMP classroom. Students should be in on the decision as to which type of supplement, if any, they work on. You should avoid giving them a sense that you are labeling them one way or the other. Let it be known that those who need reinforcement this time are not necessarily the same students that will need it next time and that all students can tackle the extension problems, not just those who the teacher feels are "capable."

Revision of Work

Students in a heterogeneous class will not vary only in their mathematics backgrounds; they will also vary in their writing ability. One way to work with these differences is to encourage revision of written work. This will benefit students who find it difficult to express ideas. Also, if a student has not solved a particular problem or completed an assignment, this will allow the student to show what he or she learned from the class discussion of the activity.

It is possible for all students to meet high standards; some simply have to work harder to get there. Opportunities to revise their work provide such students with a chance to learn from others and to improve upon their initial attempts.

Getting Students Started

For a variety of reasons, including weak English-language skills, students may sometimes have trouble getting started on an assignment. One key to getting all the students involved in a problem or activity is ensuring that each student has access to the task at hand. To give students access, you may want to have a student read the directions aloud and then have each group discuss or rewrite the task in their own words. You may throw out an open question about how to get started. You may even let the students get to work on an activity, then stop them after five minutes for group reports on where they are headed. Your goal should be to ensure that all students at least start everything you assign.

The Honors Option

A heterogeneous mathematics classroom may include students who were previously labeled "Gifted" or "Honors" and placed in separate classes. As a result, there may be parental or administrative pressure to provide an opportunity for students to have an "Honors" designation on their transcripts.

You can provide this option within your heterogeneously grouped class, offering it to every student in your IMP class, not just a select few. For example, you can have students elect to attempt some combination of the extension problems. You will need to set clear criteria for the quantity and quality of work needed for a student to receive the "Honors" designation at the end of the grading period.

You can enhance your IMP classroom by having those who do extra work make presentations to the whole class on their findings. Or you may prefer to keep this activity separate, providing regular time outside of class for students who are working on the extension problems to meet and share ideas.

Student Communication: Written and Oral Presentations

The Importance of Communication

It is vital that a member of today's society be able to communicate his or her ideas to various audiences. In business and industry, ideas are conveyed in both written and oral formats. The IMP curriculum prepares students for this need in the job market by valuing communication in the classroom. IMP students use communication every time they work on a group task, write up a homework assignment or POW, or give a presentation. They communicate through formal presentations, informal conversations, written text, diagrams, models, graphs, tables, and algebraic expressions.

Mathematics involves a special language. Because language is learned through use, IMP students benefit from a regular diet of mathematical talk as they work together on group assignments. They experience mathematical language as they read each other's written work.

Communication not only conveys information, but also provides an opportunity for teachers and peers to assess a student's thinking and depth of understanding. A piece of written work or a formal oral presentation can make clear to any audience—the small group, the whole class, or the teacher—exactly what mathematical thinking went on.

"How To's" of Oral Presentations

Getting Started

When students begin giving presentations, your first task is to get them comfortable speaking in front of a group. It may be helpful to give them some experiences addressing a partner or small group first so they can build some confidence in speaking "publicly." You will probably want your first few presentations to be on a volunteer basis, rather than by random selection, to maintain a reasonable comfort level in the classroom.

Once students have seen a few presentations, you will want to establish some method for choosing presenters that allows all students to make presentations at some time during each unit. If a particular student is extremely uncomfortable getting up in front of the class alone, you may want to allow that student to bring one or more group members along to help.

Promoting Constructive Interaction

Although you need to build students' confidence, you also can't let presenters get away with incomplete thoughts or sloppy mathematics. One tricky aspect of this—for everyone—is figuring out how to ask questions without undermining the presenter's self-esteem.

> *In 4th Year IMP: "We were working with the part of the cube unit where the kids are developing the cosine or sine of the sum of two angles. We had three visitors that day, one of whom was a language arts teacher. . . . The student at the board got to a point where she was stuck. She turned around and said that it just wasn't making any sense to her any more—she was in a state of disequilibrium. The whole class became totally focused on her dilemma. They totally took over—asking questions, answering questions, not interrupting each other. It was so hard just to sit there and do nothing. I wish we had videotaped that class. When I think of a perfect IMP class, that is the day that comes to mind. When I talked to the language arts teacher after, she said she didn't understand any of the math, but was blown away by the dynamics of what was going on in the classroom." —Jean Klanica, Eaglecrest H.S., Aurora, Colorado*

Class discussions on how to be a good audience will usually help, as will models of open-ended, clarifying questions. Have students compare constructive, nonjudgmental questions, such as "Where did the numbers in your table come from?" or "What led you to the rule you are using?" with the more intimidating "I don't understand you!" or "You don't make sense."

Good Preparation

You may get higher-quality presentations if your students prepare ahead of time. A student selected early in the week to give a POW presentation can be given pens and overhead transparencies to take home and prepare. Students may even want to practice their POW presentations with you before getting up in front of their peers.

Communication Through Writing

IMP students communicate their thoughts and ideas quite often in writing. Many assignments require the student to write out the "hows" and "whys" of a problem. Students' writing gives the teacher a window into their thoughts. IMP writing is different from the traditional math assignment, which might be just a list of answers along with number-crunching. It allows the reader to see what path the student took in solving the problem as well as the justification for traveling that path. The focus is on what the student knows and how the student knows it.

Especially with POWs, students should be encouraged to describe everything they do on a problem. At first, they may have a hard time writing about work that did not lead to a solution, even when they learned something from the effort. Sometimes students won't write anything if they did not get "the right answer." You will have to convey to them, through conversation and through your grading scheme, that the process has value even if a solution wasn't found.

Another suggestion for getting students started is to tell them to "write the way you talk." Let them know that you are interested in their ideas even if they aren't presented in perfect sentences.

Models of Excellence

Students need models to show them what good mathematics writing looks like. The best models are ones that they can relate to—work that comes from their own peers. You can provide these models by posting excellent work where they can see it. One teacher suggests making a POW write-up poster by cutting and pasting the best work from several students on different aspects of a particular problem.

Focused Free-Writing

Occasionally, the curriculum asks students to do *focused free-writing*. In this type of exercise, students are given a topic to focus on and are then asked to write for a few minutes on that topic—dumping thoughts onto paper in a stream-of-consciousness way.

The primary purpose of focused free-writing is for the student to communicate with himself or herself. Let students know ahead of time that they will not have to share their ideas if they do not want to. That will allow them to write anything that comes to mind. Since this writing is not going to be read, students don't need to worry about distractions such as grammar and spelling.

After students have finished writing, you can ask for volunteers to discuss the topic. Some students may want to read aloud from their work; others may simply share their ideas.

An Added Thought

As your students become better communicators, point out their progress to them. Let them look at the clarity and quality of their most recent POWs as compared to the first POWs of the year. Videotaping presentations so students can watch themselves may leave them pleasantly surprised by how well they did. Talk to teachers in other disciplines to hear the kudos IMP kids are receiving when they give outstanding oral reports in other classes.

Pacing in the IMP Curriculum

Fitting the Curriculum to the School Year

As you look at the IMP units, you will notice that they are broken down into "days." That is, each unit is organized into individual daily lessons, with a description of what should happen in class and what should be assigned for homework. Feedback from many teachers over the years has fine-tuned this breakdown; generally an IMP curriculum day will fit fairly well into a 50-minute class period.

You may also have noticed that, for example, each of the five Year 1 units contains about 30 days, so teaching the Year 1 curriculum exactly as outlined should take about 150 days—in theory. If your school year is 180 days, then it would seem that you have about 30 days to spare.

Enter the realities of teaching high school—fire drills, shortened assembly schedules, field trips, school-wide testing, restructured bell schedules, and teacher inservice days, to name a few. Then there is the reality that sometimes your students may not accomplish in a day what you had hoped. All of a sudden some "day" expands to a day and a half. What you will need to do is make an overall plan for the year, and then make adjustments periodically. However, you can have confidence that the overall curriculum has been adjusted, based on feedback from hundreds of classrooms, so that each "Year" of the curriculum pretty well fits a standard school year.

Concept Development and Mastery of Skills

For many teachers starting out with this curriculum, a recurrent question is "Do I need to spend more time on this topic? My students don't seem to have 'gotten it' yet. When will they see it again?"

In traditional mathematics learning, students work with each skill in isolation and are expected to master it before moving on to the next one. But students really learn in a more gradual way and the IMP curriculum takes that reality into account. It allows students to develop their understanding of concepts and their facility with skills over time and in many different contexts. The teacher's guide to each unit includes comments about the level of understanding to be expected from students at each stage of the unit's development.

Finding the Right Pace

With all that said, you still have some choices to make about the pace at which your class moves through the curriculum. Finding the right pace for your school schedule and your students will take time and experience.

You do not want to be so tied to the calendar that you breeze by topics that your students have not had sufficient time to play with and digest. If your students seem to have insight into a problem or activity, but do not meet the activity's goals, you may want to allot more class time for the assignment. On the other hand, you do not want to be drilling a topic when the goal of the unit is simply to give students an intuitive feel for an idea.

You will probably be best off if you follow the schedule for each unit fairly closely the first time you teach it. Make written notes of spots where students were quicker than the teacher's guide led you to expect, as well as of the places they were bogged down. Keep a record of things like

- how you would teach the same lesson next time

- what questions you would ask students to get them going

- how much time should really be spent

- what you could have done differently in a prior unit in order to facilitate learning in the current unit

As you pace your way through each unit, know that you and your students have the flexibility to stop and reflect on where you are in the unit and how the unit's goals are being achieved. Sometimes students tend to lose sight of the forest for the trees, doing each day's activities as if the activities were all independent of each other. By asking questions and having students reflect, you can help them make connections to the main problem or theme of the unit.

Until you have taught the four-year IMP sequence and know where topics are going, you should resist the temptation to interrupt the flow of a unit and supplement the curriculum content with your own materials. There will be times when not all of your students "see the light," as well as times that the "ah-ha" experience happens in the first 15 minutes of a two-day activity and you are left wondering what to do. If your students need more work on a concept or an added challenge in some part of the curriculum, use the supplemental problems at the end of the unit.

Nontraditional Scheduling

If your school does not have 50-minute-a-day, five-day-a-week math periods, you'll need to make some adjustments in order to fit IMP's "days" into your scheduling.

There is no simple formula for this, but the classwork/homework flow of the units should be maintained as closely as possible, especially because many in-class activities are designed with the idea that students will have each other's support as they explore new ideas. Moving a homework assignment into class time will cause less disruption of the development of the mathematics than vice versa. If you have any kind of restructured schedule, your best bet is to network with an IMP school with a similar schedule.

Calculators in the IMP Classroom

Technology in Society and Education

The world in which we live is becoming increasingly more technological:

> Today, real people in real situations regularly put finger to button and make critical decisions about which buttons to press, not where and how to carry threes into hundreds columns. We understand that this change is on the order of magnitude of the outhouse to indoor plumbing in terms of comfort and convenience, and of the sundial to digital timepieces in terms of accuracy and accessibility.[6]

Our students are headed for a job market powered by computer systems, electronic spreadsheets, numerical analyses, and computer graphics packages. It is important that they enter the world with both technological and problem-solving confidence. Today's programmable calculators are, in fact, hand-held computers.

Technology is not only an essential tool in the world of work, but it has also opened new horizons for mathematics education. The graphing calculator expedites numerical computation, graphing, matrix manipulation, statistical analysis, and many other mathematical processes, allowing students to examine and analyze mathematical topics at a deeper level.

Mathematics has traditionally been a filter in the education process, eliminating students based solely on their level of computational proficiency. The calculator helps remove that filter, breaking down the barriers to mathematical understanding and allowing students to investigate numerical patterns, efficiently test strategies, and explore the "whys." IMP does not propose abandoning computation, but instead encourages students to use the particular computational method—such as mental computation, calculator computation, or estimation—that they consider most useful for the problem being solved.

---

[6]Leinwand, Steve, "It's Time to Abandon Computational Algorithms," *Education Week*, February 9, 1994.

Calculators Always Available

Each IMP student should have a graphing calculator within arm's reach at all times during class. *At all times* means just that! For the calculator to be a natural tool for doing mathematics, the student must make the decision as to when to use it. It is not up to the teacher to decide "Today is a calculator day," or "They should not need to use calculators today." You will often be pleasantly surprised by when and how often students reach for the calculator!

Homework assignments and POWs do not require the use of a programmable graphing calculator, but students are expected to have a scientific calculator for home use. You may want to check out graphing calculators to students for home use occasionally, either for special projects or if they simply want to learn more about them.

What About Computers?

The Interactive Mathematics Program decided early in its work that it wanted every student always to have a powerful technological tool at hand. Economic realities led to the decision to build the curriculum around graphing calculators rather than computers. Thus, there are no activities in the program that require the use of a computer. There are many activities in which computer programs can provide valuable enrichment; schools that have computer labs can supplement the program with appropriate software.

Assessment and Grading

Assessment Is More than Just Grading

The words "assessment" and "grading" are sometimes used interchangeably, but it is helpful to distinguish between them.

Assessment is something you do every day as you gauge where students are in the learning process. You are assessing your students when you ask them questions, read their homework, and listen to their mathematical conversations. These assessments guide your instructional decisions regarding pacing, teaching strategies, and "where to go from here." Getting as accurate a reading as possible requires that students be observed and assessed in real situations; hence the term *authentic assessment*, which is used frequently in educational reform.

Assessment should be part of the ongoing educational process and should enhance learning. Unlike the standardized tests, which create a break in learning in order to take a measurement, assessment should be part of the natural flow of the classroom. When the curriculum provides a window into a student's thinking, that is a natural time to assess that student. Such an assessment need not be something you assign a specific grade to—it may be simply for informational purposes, both for you and for the student.

How Does Grading Fit In?

In a sense, grading is one of the by-products of assessment. As teachers, we have the responsibility of assigning each student a grade periodically throughout the year. Somehow, you must determine a grade—usually a single letter or number—to reflect all of a student's performance in one lump sum. Not a simple task!

The first step in deciding of how to grade your IMP students is to sit down and decide what you really value in your IMP classroom. Some of the following may come to mind:

- Completion of homework

- Group and class participation

- Progress in the concepts and skills of the unit

- Mathematical communication through written work and oral presentations

These are broad goals; your task is to construct a grading scheme that reflects your priorities.

One way to construct a grading scheme is by allocating "value dollars." Imagine that you have 100 value dollars to spend. Write down the four or five aspects of student work that you value most and apportion your value dollars accordingly.

The list should reflect your personal priorities as well as school policies, and you may find that your allotment changes from year to year. For example, I started with the following "budget":

Homework assignments	$30
Problems of the Week	$20
Oral presentations	$20
Write-ups of class activities	$20
End-of-unit assessments	$10

Your own choices may be different. The discussion below concerning end-of-unit assessments will help explain why you might assign them only $10, compared to the traditional practice of giving major weight to final tests. Teachers find that working out these decisions together gives them all confidence in their choices, even if they disagree.

Once you've created such a list, you can then use it to assign percentages in your grading scheme. As you become more familiar with the IMP curriculum, your values may change; your grading policy should reflect such change.

Whatever system you use, it is vital that your students be informed about the grading process. Students should know where their grade is coming from. They should know what is valued and should have ways to participate in the process.

What Assignments to Grade

Although assessment is taking place every day in your IMP classroom, you will need specific tools for assigning grades. Since you can't thoroughly read and comment on all the work your students do, you need to make some choices. The overview section of each teacher's guide suggests a specific selection of assignments that represent progress toward the unit's goals.

These suggestions use a balance of activities, including assignments that focus on specific skills as well as those in which students can demonstrate a broad understanding of the development of concepts. They are spread throughout the unit and include both in-class and at-home work.

End-of-Unit Assessments

There are both an in-class and a take-home "assessment" at the end of most units. These end-of-unit assessments should be just one tool of many in your grading tool kit. They are not intended to "cover" the unit, but rather to give students a chance to show some of what they have learned. You may decide that some of the supplemental problems also make good assessment tools.

The in-class assessments are intentionally quite short. You should give students the whole class period, even though most of them will need less time. That will allow you to measure how well—not how fast—students reason, think, and communicate.

Grades and End-of-Unit Assessments

Perhaps an extra word is in order about the role of end-of-unit assessments in grading.

Many of us have sometimes used end-of-chapter tests as the primary tool for grading, but we've also had the experience of seeing a "top" student do poorly on such a test. When that happens to me, I generally conclude that the student simply had a bad day and I assign a grade based on my broader knowledge of the student. In other words, I trust the judgments that I have built up over an extensive period of observation more than I trust the results of a single test.

This principle applies even more with the IMP curriculum, because you have so many opportunities to evaluate your students' work. Keep in mind that the end-of-unit assessments represent perhaps two hours of student work in a unit that may have involved twenty to thirty hours of class time and many more hours of homework.

Some "How To's" to Help with Grading

Once you have made the decision as to *what* you are going to grade, you need to figure out *how* to get it graded. Of course, the first step is to work the problem or do the activity yourself to appreciate its complexities and difficulties. If possible, discuss it with a colleague.

Here are some other tips gathered from experienced IMP teachers.

Grading Problems of the Week

POW grading is most efficiently done holistically. Holistic scoring means developing an overall sense of how well the student has done, rather than focusing on specific details. Many teachers do this by sorting papers into piles according to a broad standard (sometimes called a *rubric*). The teacher reads through the papers, focusing on explanation of process and solution, and puts each paper into one of the piles.

Many teachers use three basic piles—*above the standard*, *meets the standard*, and *not acceptable*. You might then subdivide each pile into two, and use that final sorting to assign grades. By reading student work with a focus and by limiting comments on the student papers, you can grade a class set of POWs in a reasonable amount of time.

Grading Homework

There is not enough time in the day to thoroughly grade every piece of student homework that comes in. Most experienced IMP teachers grade the bulk of homework according to completion. This can be done by stamping the homework or marking it off in your grade book as students come into class. In order to build in more accountability on occasion, you can focus on one particular part of the assignment or ask a specific question to gauge how students did.

Grading Group Participation

As you observe groups working, you will be getting insight into how well they are able to share the tasks they are assigned, and can give the group as a whole a grade on its members' ability to collaborate.

You may also find it helpful to have group members grade each other periodically on participation. You might have students do some self-reflection and grade themselves as participants in their groups. Students are typically very honest. In fact, many are too hard on themselves, so you will want to reserve the right to raise self-assigned scores.

Grading Group Projects

Occasionally, you may need to assign grades to projects or investigations done by each group as a whole. The simplest approach is to assign the same grade to each group member.

As an alternative, you can give a lump sum to the group and have group members decide how to allocate it. For example, suppose you want to allow each student a maximum of 10 points on a given assignment, which would be a total of 40 points for a four-person group. If the group did *B* work, you might give them 34 points and have the group divide the total among themselves (and justify their decision).

Changing Over Time

As you become more experienced in teaching IMP, you will develop a system that works for you. Take time out occasionally to assess your grading scheme to make sure it reflects what you value. Also make sure it is doable—the profession needs you, so don't burn yourself out trying to be "Superreader"! Be selective in what you grade and stay on the lookout for the most effective and efficient way to get it done.

Portfolios

What Is a Portfolio?

At the end of each IMP unit, each student is asked to write a cover letter reflecting on the mathematics of the unit. Students also select samples from their work in the unit, both to represent their own learning and to demonstrate how specific activities contributed to the overall development of mathematical ideas. In the process of assembling the portfolio, the student has the opportunity to synthesize what he or she has learned.

This material, and perhaps some other reflective writing, is put together to form the student's portfolio for the unit. A more creative portfolio may include a videotape of an experiment or presentation, or photographs of student products or experiences, as well as written work. Group products may be photocopied so more than one group member can use them.

The individual unit portfolios together form a growing picture of the student's learning. The portfolios serve as a demonstration of both the student's progress and the instructional program for parents and administrators. Questions regarding a student's progress can be answered by reading through that student's work, thoughts, and reflections. The portfolio is much more informative than a set of test scores!

Using Portfolios

Students' portfolios can serve them as they continue their mathematics education. They can look back into their portfolio to refresh their knowledge of a topic from their own point of view. For example, students working on *Do Bees Build It Best?* (a Year 2 unit) may be a bit rusty on the trigonometric functions. Students can go back into their portfolios from *Shadows* (a Year 1 unit) to look at initial findings on sine, cosine, and tangent from their own perspectives. Many students have sent along portions of their IMP portfolios as part of their college applications.

Teachers have a variety of policies on grading portfolios. Some teachers look for completeness, since the bulk of the samples put into the portfolios have already been graded. Others assign a grade based on demonstration of student growth or understanding, especially as reflected in the cover letter. However you choose to grade the portfolios, you should use them for a broader kind of assessment from time to time. Both you and the students should take time to look through the portfolios and get a feel for areas of growth and, perhaps, areas of need.

The portfolio should be available to students for use or revision at all times. Teachers have found it convenient to have the student portfolios in folders hanging either in a filing cabinet or in a crate in the classroom. Year 1 portfolios follow the student into Year 2. Some schools turn portfolios over to students to keep at home when Year 2 begins.

Day-to-Day Stuff

As we deal with the big picture—the reform of mathematics education to meet the needs of the twenty-first century—we need the help and encouragement of our colleagues. Here is an assortment of tips from the experiences of many teachers who have been successfully implementing the IMP curriculum and enjoying it.

Handling Materials

The first IMP unit, *Patterns,* includes a list of the general supplies that are needed throughout the four-year program. Supplies that are needed only for a particular unit are listed in the overview for that unit.

You can ease management of materials by having a bucket, bowl, or bin for each group. This container should hold the daily necessities—calculators, overhead pens, blank transparencies, a couple of felt markers, rulers, protractors, scissors, and anything specific to the unit or lesson being taught, such as dice or pendulum-building supplies. You can keep the buckets on the tables or else store them in some common area where, say, the "heart card students" from each group will be responsible for picking them up at the beginning of class and returning them at the end.

If you are using materials that need to be locked up at the end of class, such as stopwatches, make sure you leave a few minutes at the end of class to count and collect them. You may want to put a student in charge of letting you know when there are five minutes left in class so you can collect materials and assign the homework. Occasional class discussions on the value of the technology and manipulatives may be necessary to deter theft or vandalism.

Calculator Management and Security

Having calculators available at all times creates a need for a management system. Your goal is to have some system that results in your class set of graphing calculators' sitting on the groups' tables as soon as they enter your classroom. (You will be amazed at how much today's technologically adept young people will learn about the calculator by "hacking around" before and after the bell rings!) You might want to use the same containers in which you keep the other daily materials. The important thing to remember is to make it as convenient as possible for the students to access the calculators; if students have to get up out of their seats and walk across the room to get one, they may opt not to!

The security of the calculators may or may not be an issue for your classroom. If you are concerned about the safety of your class set of calculators, you should develop a management system that ensures that all calculators are accounted for at the beginning and end of class, without impeding their accessibility. An integral part of any calculator management system must be ongoing communication with the students about what a privilege it is to have real-world mathematical tools and how important the calculators are to the IMP classroom.

One calculator management system involves labeling the calculators with the symbols by which you randomly group your students. For example, if you assign your students to groups using playing cards, you could tape a playing card on the back of each calculator. Taping a card or label on the back of the calculator so that it covers the battery case can also deter the unwanted removal of the batteries.

No matter what kind of system you develop for ensuring the safety of the calculators, make sure that your students are part of your system. They need to be included in the decision that the calculators are an invaluable tool that they cannot afford to lose.

Getting Good Attendance

Of course, no curriculum program or teaching strategy will solve the problem of absenteeism, but this issue is especially important in the IMP classroom, where student interaction plays such an important role in learning.

Fortunately, the emphasis on group collaboration also provides one potential solution to the problem. Hold class discussions to bring out the fact that group work functions best when all group members are present. Make each student feel that his or her presence is valued *every day*. Give group members the responsibility for getting each other to class.

Encourage students to call each other after being absent to see what was missed. Avoid answering the question "I wasn't here yesterday, what did I miss?" Simply respond, "Ask your group." Students should do any homework that was assigned while they were out. Making up class activities might require the student to come in before or after school with other absentees or to do the activity alone. Students can often pick up details from group members and from later activities.

Motivating Students to Do Homework and POWs

Like absence, this is an issue in many classrooms, but in IMP, the assignments are not just practice of what was done in class that day, and they often provide essential preparation for the following day. This makes it vital that students do their homework regularly.

There is no magic elixir that you can give your students to make them do their homework every night. You can try some of the following suggestions, though:

- Hold discussions on the role of homework in the IMP curriculum.

- Use your grading system to show the value you place on homework and POWs. Some students need external recognition for doing the work. If you never collect the work or acknowledge students for having done it, they may tend to slack off.

- If students do not complete an assignment, have them write a letter either to you or to their parents explaining why. This will not only tell you about legitimate excuses, such as a family emergency, but may help you adjust your teaching or give you something to use when you call or meet with the student's parents regarding the noncompletion of homework.

- Reward groups all of whose members turn in their homework.

- Have students read their fellow group members' work. This not only adds peer pressure to yours, but also gives students an opportunity to learn from each other.

- Have group members phone each other to remind them of assignments due or past due. You can use phone calls yourself to let students know about their good work.

Conclusion

If you are an experienced teacher, but new to IMP, you doubtless have formed many insights that will apply to your teaching of the IMP curriculum, and you probably recognized many ideas in this handbook that you have already used in a traditional mathematics classroom. Some of you may have been drawn to IMP in the first place because it supports what you have been doing or what you have been trying to do. If you are a new teacher, perhaps some of these suggestions will help you in the first challenging weeks. In either case, the collegial support of hundreds of IMP teachers accompanies you into your IMP classroom, and the successes of thousands of IMP students await your students. Welcome to an adventure!

Appendix: IMP Curriculum Summary

Year 1

Patterns

The primary purpose of this unit is to introduce students to ways of working on and thinking about mathematics that may be new to them. In a sense, the unit is an overall introduction to the Interactive Mathematics Program, which for many students involves changes in how they learn mathematics and what they think of as mathematics. In this unit, major emphasis is placed on developing the ability to think about and explore mathematical problems.

Some important mathematical ideas and concepts are introduced and worked with in this unit, especially function tables, the use of variables, positive and negative numbers, and some basic geometrical concepts.

Another major theme is the idea of proof. This is not developed as a formal process but rather as part of the larger theme of reasoning and explaining. Students' ability to create and understand proofs will develop over the course of the four-year IMP curriculum; their work in this unit is just a beginning.

The Game of Pig

A dice game called Pig forms the core of this unit. Playing and analyzing Pig involves students in a wide variety of mathematical activities. The basic problem for students is to find an optimal strategy for playing the game. In order to find a good strategy and prove that it is optimal, students work with the concept of expected value and develop a mathematical analysis of the game based on an area model for probability. They can also use a computer to simulate both Pig and a simpler version of the game, so that they can compare strategies and check the theoretical probabilities experimentally.

Probabilistic thinking frequently runs counter to our intuitions. For this reason, the activities in this unit are based in concrete experiences. Students' belief in luck is terribly persistent; it takes a great deal of experience before they become willing to base their predictions on probabilistic notions. The gambler's fallacy—that the next roll of the dice depends on previous rolls—is held with conviction even by well-informed adults. One goal of this unit is for students to recognize this fallacy, both in dice games and in real-life situations. More broadly, they will come to understand theoretical probability and to see how and when it can be used to model and give insight into situations that occur every day.

The Overland Trail

This unit looks at the mid–nineteenth century western migration across the United States in terms of the many linear relationships involved. These relationships grow out of the study of planning what to take on the 2,400-mile trek, estimating the cost of the move, and studying rates of consumption and of travel.

Students construct mathematical models and draw graphs by hand and with a graphing calculator. They interpret graphs in terms of the "stories" the graphs tell, and create graphs from "stories." They write algebraic expressions that represent situations, use manipulatives to represent variables, and solve systems of equations using graphs made by hand and by a function-graphing facility on a calculator. In the process of graphing equations, they see the need to solve equations for one variable in terms of another, and learn techniques for doing so.

The Pit and the Pendulum

This unit opens with an excerpt from *The Pit and the Pendulum*, by Edgar Allan Poe. In the story, a prisoner is tied down while a pendulum with a sharp blade slowly descends. If the prisoner does not act, he will be killed by the pendulum. When the pendulum has about 12 swings left, the prisoner creates a plan for escape and executes it. Students are presented with the problem of whether the prisoner would have enough time to escape. To resolve this question, students construct pendulums and conduct experiments to find out what variables determine the length of the period of a pendulum and what the relationship is between the period and these variables.

In the process, students are introduced to the normal distribution and the standard deviation as tools for determining whether a change in one variable really does affect another. They make and refine conjectures, analyze data collected from experiments, and use graphing calculators to learn about quadratic equations and to explore curve fitting. Finally, after deriving a theoretical answer to the problem, students actually build a 30-foot pendulum to test their theory.

Shadows

This unit opens with the question, "How can you predict the length of a shadow?" Students experiment with flashlights to isolate the important variables and try to predict the length of the shadow in terms of one of those variables. They are told that in order to understand shadows and the data they have found, they need to learn some geometry.

Students work with a variety of concrete objects to come to an understanding of similar polygons, especially similar triangles. They then return to the problem of the shadow, applying their knowledge of similar triangles and using informal methods for solving proportions to develop a general formula. In the last part of the unit, students learn about the three primary trigonometric functions—sine, cosine, and tangent—as they are defined for acute angles, and apply these functions to problems of finding heights and distances.

Year 2

Solve It!

This unit focuses on using equations to represent real-life situations and on developing the skills to solve these equations. Students begin with situations used in the first year of the curriculum and develop algebraic representations of problems. In order to find solutions to the equations that arise, students explore the concepts of equivalent expressions and equivalent equations.

Using these concepts, they learn principles such as the distributive property for working with algebraic expressions and equations, and acquire methods that they can use to solve any linear equation. They also explore the relationships among an algebraic expression, a function, an equation, and a graph, and examine ways to use graphs to solve nonlinear equations.

Is There Really a Difference?

In this unit, students collect data and compare different population groups to one another. In particular, they concentrate on the following question:

> If a sample from one population differs in some respect from
> a sample from a different population, how reliably can you
> infer that the overall populations differ in that respect?

They begin by making double bar graphs of some classroom data, then explore the process of making and testing hypotheses. Students realize that there is variation even among different samples from the same population, and see the usefulness of the concept of a null hypothesis as they examine this variation. They build on their understanding of the standard deviation from the Year 1 unit *The Pit and the Pendulum*, and learn that the chi-square (χ^2) statistic can give them the probability of seeing differences of a certain size between samples when the populations are really the same.

Their work in this unit culminates in a two-week project, in which they propose a hypothesis about two populations that they think really differ in some respect. They then collect sample data about the two populations and analyze their data using bar graphs, tables, and the χ^2 statistic.

Do Bees Build It Best?

In this unit, students work on the following problem:

> Bees store their honey in honeycombs that consist of cells they make out of wax. What is the best design for a honeycomb?

To analyze this problem, students begin by learning about area and the Pythagorean theorem. Then, using the Pythagorean theorem and trigonometry, they find a formula for the area of a regular polygon with fixed perimeter, and find that the larger the number of sides, the larger the area of the polygon.

Students then turn their attention to volume and surface area, focusing on prisms whose bases are regular polygons. They find that for such prisms, if they also want the honeycomb cells to fit together, the mathematical winner, in terms of maximizing volume for a given surface area, is a regular hexagonal prism, which is essentially the choice of the bees.

Cookies

This unit focuses on graphing systems of linear inequalities and solving systems of linear equations. Although the central problem is in the field of linear programming, the major goal of the unit is for students to learn how to manipulate equations and how to reason using graphs.

Students begin by considering a classic type of linear programming problem, in which they are asked to maximize the profits of a cookie store that makes plain and iced cookies. They are constrained by the amounts of ingredients they have on hand and the amounts of oven time and labor time available.

First students work toward a graphical solution of the problem. They see how the linear function can be maximized or minimized by studying the graph. Since the maximum or minimum point that they are looking for is often at the intersection of two lines, they are motivated to investigate a method for solving two equations in two unknowns.

They then return to work in groups on the cookie problem; each group presents both a solution and a proof that its solution does maximize profits. Finally, each group invents its own linear programming problem and makes a presentation of the problem and its solution to the class.

All About Alice

This unit starts with a model based on Lewis Carroll's *Alice in Wonderland*, in which Alice's height is doubled or halved by her eating or drinking certain magical items. Out of the discussion of this situation come the basic principles for working with exponents—positive, negative, zero, and even fractional—and an introduction to logarithms.

Building on the work with exponents, the unit covers scientific notation and the manipulation of numbers written in scientific notation.

Year 3

Fireworks

The central problem of this unit involves sending up rockets to create a fireworks display. The trajectory of the rocket is a parabola; this unit continues the algebraic investigations of *Solve It!* with a special focus on quadratic expressions, equations, and functions. Students see that they can use algebra to find the vertex of the graph of a quadratic function by writing the quadratic expression in a particular form.

Orchard Hideout

The central problem of this unit concerns a couple who have planted an orchard on a circular lot. They want to know how long it will take before the trees grow large enough to hide the center of the orchard from the outside world. Answering this question requires students to study circles and coordinate geometry. They develop the formulas for the circumference and the area of a circle, as well as the distance and midpoint formulas, and learn to find the distance from a point to a line. Another theme of the unit is geometric proof.

Throughout this unit, students are applying knowledge they acquired in earlier units about similar triangles, trigonometry, and the Pythagorean theorem.

Meadows or Malls?

The title problem of this unit concerns a decision that must be made about land use. This problem can be expressed using a system of linear inequalities, which lends itself to a solution by means of linear programming, a topic introduced in the Year 2 unit *Cookies*. Building on their work in that unit, students see that a key step in solving the system of linear inequalities is to find various points of intersection of the graphs of the corresponding equations. This in turn leads to the need to solve systems of linear equations. Along the way, students learn about graphing equations in three variables, see that the graph of a linear equation in three variables is a plane, and study the possible intersections of planes in space.

Because graphing calculators allow students to find inverses of square matrices (when the inverses exist), matrices are a good tool for solving systems of linear equations with several variables. So in addition to strengthening their skills with traditional methods, students learn to express linear systems in terms of matrices and develop the matrix operations required to understand the role of matrices in the solution process.

Small World, Isn't It?

This unit opens with a table of world population data over the last several centuries; it asks this rather facetious question:

> If population growth continues to follow this pattern,
> how long will it be until people are squashed up against
> each other?

In order to attack this problem, students study a variety of situations involving rates of growth. Based on these examples, they develop the concept of slope, and then generalize this to the idea of the derivative, the instantaneous rate of growth. In studying derivatives numerically, they discover that an exponential function has the special property that its derivative is proportional to the value of the function, and see that, intuitively, population growth functions ought to have a similar property. This, together with simplified growth models, suggests that an exponential function is a reasonable choice to use to approximate their population data.

They also learn that every exponential function can be expressed in terms of any positive base (except 1) and that scientists use as a standard basis the number for which the derivative of the exponential function equals the value of the function. They find this base, e, experimentally. Along the route of their study of exponential functions, they review logarithms, are introduced to the natural log function, and see that logarithms are a useful tool for answering questions raised by exponential functions.

Pennant Fever

One team has a three-game lead over its closest rival for the baseball pennant. Each team has seven games to go in the season (none of which are between these two teams). The central problem of the unit is to find the probability that the team that is leading will win the pennant.

Students use the teams' current records to set up a probability model for the problem. Their analysis of that model requires an understanding of combinatorial coefficients and uses the tool of probability tree diagrams. In the course of their analysis, students work through the general topic of permutations and combinations, and develop the binomial theorem and properties of Pascal's triangle. Their general understanding of the binomial distribution is also applied to several decision problems involving statistical reasoning.

Year 4

High Dive

The central problem of this unit involves a circus act in which a diver will fall from a turning Ferris wheel into a tub of water that is on a moving cart. The students' task is to determine when the diver should be released from the Ferris wheel in order to land in the moving tub of water.

The geometry of the Ferris wheel generates the need to express the diver's position in terms of the angle through which the Ferris wheel has turned. Students are led to extend right-triangle trigonometric functions to the circular functions. They learn about the graphs of the sine and cosine functions and apply them both to geometric situations and to other contexts. In particular, they see how the graph of a sine-like function changes as various parameters such as period and amplitude are changed.

Students then study the physics of falling objects and develop an algebraic expression for the time of the diver's fall in terms of his position. They also have to take into account the diver's initial velocity, which is imparted by the movement of the Ferris wheel itself. Therefore, they must learn how to analyze the diver's motion in terms of its vertical and horizontal components.

Along the way, students are introduced to several additional trigonometric concepts, such as polar coordinates, inverse trigonometric functions, and the Pythagorean identity.

As the Cube Turns

This unit opens with an overhead display, generated by a program on a graphing calculator. The two-dimensional display depicts the rotation of a cube in three-dimensional space. The students' central task in the unit is to learn how to write such a program.

Though the task is defined in terms of writing a program, the real focus of the unit is the mathematics behind the program. The unit takes students into several areas of mathematics. They study the fundamental geometric transformations—translations, rotations, and reflections—in both two and three dimensions, and express them in terms of coordinates. The analysis of rotations builds on the experience they have just had in *High Dive* with trigonometric functions and polar coordinates, and leads them to see the need for and to develop formulas for the sine and cosine of the sum of two angles. Working with these transformations also provides a new setting in which students can work with matrices, which they previously studied in connection with systems of linear equations.

Another complex component of their work is the analysis of how to represent a three-dimensional object on a two-dimensional screen. They have an opportunity to see how projection onto a plane is affected by both the choice of the plane and the choice of a viewpoint or center of projection.

The unit closes with two major projects, which students work on in pairs: They write a program to make the cube turn and they program an animated graphic display of their own design.

Know How

This unit is designed to prepare students to find out independently about mathematical content that they either have not learned or have forgotten. Most will need this skill in later education as well as in their adult work lives. Students who come through a nontraditional curriculum, such as the IMP, may need to fill in knowledge to meet expectations established for traditional programs.

Students are given experiences of learning through traditional textbooks and through interviewing others. The content explored this way includes radian measure, ellipses, the quadratic formula, the laws of sines and cosines, and complex numbers.

The World of Functions

This unit builds on students' extensive previous work with functions. They explore some basic families of functions (linear, quadratic, polynomials in general, exponential, sine-like, logarithmic, reciprocal, rational functions in general, and power functions) in terms of various representations—their tables, their graphs,

their algebraic
used to model.

Students use funct
They see that find
sometimes involves
times requires insigh

Then students explo
representations, using
conclude the unit by re
unit *Small World, Isn't*
find a function that fits
ones they used in the thir

The Pollster's Dilemma

The central limit theorem
sampling. Through a variety
process of sampling, with a s
sample affects the variation in sa

The opening problem concerns
the voters favoring a certain candi
confident should the candidate be

Students conduct sampling experim
there is a theoretical probability dis
sample of a given size. They review
Pennant Fever to see how to find the

By experimentation, they see that the r
given size are approximately normally
the statement of the central limit theo
experimental observation. Building on w
Pit and the Pendulum, students lear
distributions and standard deviations to fi
They also see how concepts such as marg
reporting polling results.

In addition to putting the new concepts
problem, students work in pairs on a sampling
of their own. They write reports and make pr
how they chose their sample size and what their